love letters to love

ABOUT THE COVER

The cover for this chapbook took quite a while to create-
mostly because I knew exactly what I wanted to put on it, and
had to spare a fair amount of time researching! It had to be
fitting to the theme of the poems, but not so complicated that it
distracted from them. Flowers- and flower language - were the
answer.
In no particular order, here are the flowers featured on the
front cover of *love letters to love*:

MAIDENHAIR FERN - a secret love, romantic fascination
FORGET-ME-NOT - true love and remembrance
WILD HONEYSUCKLE - joy and devoted love
SWEET PEA - gratitude and departure

And of course, the back cover of the print version features
violets. You, dear reader, can draw your own meanings from
that.

I want a love that will shape my life.
love that will shake my life,
settle my foundations, mine out the root
of my house the soft gold the gleaming gems
polish the war-weathered steel of my life, like surgery
love to hollow my bones like a bird,
to bring me down to the deepest that there is.

o love, you unfickle god used for our own ends
you white-wrapped child, you red-robed wife!
o love, you heavy-hearted husband of ill and well,
you carrier of torches, you spinner of silence,
you watcher of the river-drowned men scorned!

(The poet rests.)

O love! Finish what you began.
Grow old in the house you built with your two hands,
abused with the hammer and nail though
you placed each board with tenderness.
It is the same tenderness that held your first-born child,
the hands that laid your parents in their grave.

This was the last memory I had of him: resting in a tower of golden light. All covered in stories and words- poems and love stories and adventures and alchemists' shopping lists- knowledge in every written language, text covering every inch of him.

He did not write love over his heart but mercy, and justice, and knowledge- all precious things- these words in the French language, which they say is the language of romantics. He wrote love over each eye instead.

"I want to see love in this world," he said.

When I traced the unreadable lines across his ribs he said it was a medical text that had since been lost to the fires- one day it would be copied from his body, he promised, and smiled as though that was all he wanted in the entire world.

I translated instead the poem inscribed in the shadow of his throat and the hollows of his collarbones. It cannot be written here- I no longer know the words.

One panel across his hip was so black with letters that I could hardly see the skin, so covered with line upon line following the muscle and the bone.

He was no less marked than the rest of his kind, those people who treat knowledge as sacred. I know through their lives the followers of that order write their knowledge on their skin to take with them into the next life.

It's said they're sought after as lovers, and that there is no secret like their secrets- warm words in places they show nearly no one.

But he shared so freely that I could hardly believe the stories at all. A library of a man, covered in lovely words and knowledge no longer spoken.

It has come to OUR ESTEEMED ATTENTION that you have been
doing wonderful things,
SUCH AS IN THE FOLLOWING:
rising in the mornings when it is time to rise;
washing your face, which WE find very beautiful;
dressing in the manner you prefer, which WE believe most
appealing;
attending dinner with OUR ESTEEMED SELF;
existing in the particular space and time which permits US to greet
you;
placing your hands around OUR waist, yet removing them when
asked;
maintaining a state of pleasant feelings on occasion, which
pleases US greatly;

IN GREAT APPRECIATION of your continued efforts, WE extend
a CORDIAL INVITATION to OUR personal chambers.
YOUR ESTEEMED PRESENCE is requested beginning between
the hours of 7 and 9 in the evening.
Refreshments, sleeping accommodations, and bedclothes are all
to be provided at YOUR express preference.

If you would like to accept OUR INVITATION,
leave your hat on the WOODEN BENCH in the park nearest to
your house.
It will be returned when you arrive.

HOLDING

I wanted to write something gentle
something small and full of
the soft dim heat of hand on cheek
child and mother nestled in sleep

I want to create a silver word mirror
the world is full of gentle light–
you are here, and here, and you are not vanishing–
and that too is a warm and precious thing–

II.

-you must not forget the words, she said to me this evening in the autumn light. It was gentle on our skin, like some transparent type of clothing that draped over her breasts and settled around our legs. Her skin looked to be covered by thousands of precious pearl beads, all the letters gone unreadable and strange in the dimness and the light.

-but what are the words? I asked.

-any of them, she said. all of them. every whisper of yours is sacred.

I had never been so loved as to be sacred before. I didn't know what to do. When I told her that she laughed and said-

-that too is sacred.

Then she kissed me again, and I had no words.

I can see how it was worshipped as the height of love
in these cold days, although I am wanting,
I find myself longing for your sweet touch;
though I stand by the fire, your body held the greater warmth.
My dear one, this love of love that you describe as absolute-
I wish for your happiness.
Is it selfishness to wish that you have all your desires?
In a dream you chose me over and over again.

AN OLD MAP FROM THE BOTTOM OF THE DRAWER

I would rather the world map skin memory
etch in joy love hope on my heart streets
tell who where what discovered
this home a lover and past the hills another;
here tree where we traded name small kiss hope touch;
there is the city my child learned to walk;
this is the place my voice first learned to sing.

my dear, if you want a love song, don't go to the markets.
Don't listen to the musicians of the sweet tea houses;
spare a coin for street singers, but don't stop to hear.
Wait for a night when the moon is thin and starving
        a waning moon will hold forth a sad song;
        a waxing moon will pour out a hopeful one.
Wait outside on a night neither cloudless nor clouded,
near a home whose stones are still warm from the sun.

This is the place where the girls sing their love songs, the
half-dream
where women go to know things that no mortal understands.
This is the lady moon who teaches their hearts that music,
who holds their night-secrets and does not wipe their tears
for any reason; you'll find songs in the sorrow and the light.

AS I HOLD YOUR HOLY BODY IN MY ARMS

my love, not all poetry must be said aloud; look:
hand on chest, bare warm echo chamber
empty rise and strain
architecture hollow arches
a thrum and a beat; breathe
and raise your own cathedral.
the smallest of drums a gentle the size of your fist;
on exhale: no words.

gentle and fond
affection an old sweater flannel soft / a blanket /
warm plaid rough on cheek on palm skin / curls feather soft
fingertips to lashes barely there fringe promises of sleep

deity / sunlight on skin mortal knowing / tomorrow /
tomorrow / not today / morning
sun light caressing beloved
gaze awed bright precious / precious / beloved

oh wonder of wonders my love / you are beloved
/ you are a sacred place
my heart stands besides me /
my heart walks besides me.

and maybe I should write violets-
I can talk about the petals, the dark softness
how touching them is a metaphor
I can make each curve fragile and compare to the palm of your
breasts
which are delicate like flowers and soft to touch-

but we are not only made of these things.
sometimes skin is only skin and skin-hunger a kind of tragedy
more evocative than the old epics (who can relate to those?)
more evocative all we have been afraid to touch
afraid to be touched and I write best the places I have been to

darling, give me a flower. make my body fragile, fleeting, thorned-
my love make me a tree, strong and shelter.
let's be ethereal like dryads let's be goddesses
let's forget here now we have real bodies
and real skin, real awkward and jutting bones and aches and pains.
let me write violets which I have never held and never seen.

my hands are cold
numb fingers ice sticks flesh
i imagine touching your face and can't feel it
cold inside and out
imagine you flinching back from touch

like Sappho i can say nothing
like Sappho i despair over loveliness

look down

        saying nothing

PURCHASING A POTION OF LOVE

In fairy tales, all things come in threes.
The first time I tell you this true thing (that I love you)
you will not know me or my heart from which it comes.
The second time, you will see and hear me although
you will not believe my words. This too is the way of star-crossed
lovers.
The third time I tell you I love you you will know the words;
you may take them for yourself, for they are yours.
There will be no fourth time. Some true things need not be spoken;
this is a love spell, not something we understand.

III.

I am not ashamed to say I was seduced by his body as much as his knowledge. As he would say, they are all the same thing to him... And I think that man would know, he with esoteric arts recorded along his thighs and apocrypha spread from his arms to his fingertips.

We met at the university, of course. He and his associates were a common fixture there, paying their way by assisting professors with lessons and librarians with errands and students with essays and theses.

It took longer than you might think for our relationship to escalate. For one, though we were the same in age, I was a student of the university, and he however unofficially employed by it. For two, I must say that the rumors are not entirely accurate; he was not particularly eager for a partner, nor were his friends particularly approving of our little tryst when all was said and done. It seems they'd been warned to be very careful how they approached those at the university, for fear that they might be forced to leave and lose what knowledge they were seeking (although I know nothing of what that was).

At any rate, once I had moved on from what classes he appeared in, we spent the night with each other. I have not had such an attentive lover before or since, and though I am married now I dare say I never will. His hands were gentle, his arms strong, his skin soft somehow despite the hard-edged words and lines that covered it. He was all too pleased to tell me stories in languages I will likely never hear again, and use that same sweet mouth to kiss me until neither of us could hardly speak.

He has since moved on, but the morning-poem he left is one of my most prized possessions. Not one I would show a stranger, you understand. But I think I see some of the appeal of their people now, for that memory is one of my dearest and most precious, and it is a gentle knowledge that I will hold for the rest of my life.

if I am reminded of anyone I am reminded of my dreams:
of dreams I can't remember, of storms that gather in my wake
and ungather silent as I wake;
winter's first snowfall, and the autumn light
gold one last time against the people and the trees.
Here from the window everything is silence;
the illusory peace a temptress (how beautiful he is!)
Here in autumn's wake and autumn's wake
I watch the autumn leaves; I dream of thee.

This is how it goes:
I will love you when you wake,
before you put on your crown and your suit of armor.
I will love the monarch you are when you have donned them.
I will love you with tangled hair and sleep-wet eyes
and the heat of your body by me when we rest.
I will love you veiled and covered, and I will love you
on the day you reveal yourself again.
I will love you when you speak and in your silence.

I love you. I love you.
I love you here or there, away or next to me.

I love you. Please be free.

you ask me if love is like this:
a feeling of being devoured
all consuming   encompassing
a compass that won't can't point north never

but if love eats you alive then who will I love after?
if love destroys the poem-

                    my love. where have you gone?
                        Where is the poem?

IV

I never knew until the end. Not that I wasn't curious but she was one among many, and in these days who can say that not all they meet are not a little strange? If she was hungry for knowledge so were we, and hungrier for something like a human presence, companionship, a human understanding. We all had some different reason, some different mix, so we let it be.

We grew close in those halcyon days, side by side, hand in hand. And she blossomed, unfolding with some graceless unportented joy, spinning out and open like skirts in the summer dance.

How strange the day I entered and saw her in the nude! She was shy about her body, but that was only proper. More unusual were the ones who came and hardly covered themselves, shameless, basking in the horror and awe and secret jealousy of all who dared to watch. But that day she was fully bare and glowing, skin dark and rosy and the sharp needle moving across her shy face, her sweet face that I so loved. Her smile was barely upturned, tucked away, but there was nothing of shame in the visage before me. Only joy, and the long text we had so studied in long nights and longer days- the words we both knew so well- a treatise on love.

USING THE THESAURUS

i love you
my single self soul // love you
i love // soft beautiful sunbeam light
i // cherish precious awe in wonder // you
oh enter into the joyful union of time //
to beloved // to be loved.

may it be, my heart
a light in your hands,
my love
a lantern to guide you home

wherever you go a thread
(light and light and never dimming)
around your infinite fingers
tying through your subtle hair

may there always be grass beneath your feet skies
above your head wind to tell
you of everything you
are beloved

wherever you go may there be joy in your heart sun
through the rain light
through your precious hands someone to guide you home

may you always have my blessing recipient
of love you are beloved

sadness without pain:
a home I no longer belong to.

dewdrops on branches
promise made impossible by time;
lover left behind;
you are a sky I will not return to.

My love, move on.
Even the birds fly north when it's time for spring.

(...) but of all the things I have done wrong and all that I have not, I have done this right:

I love you and I have loved you and out of that love we have grown and cherished so many wonderful days.

And my love for you is not silent, and my love for you cannot be undone - not by time, nor by distance, nor by lovers, nor by leaving.

Whatever happens from here on, my darling, you have already known all of me. And if my body does not come home, my heart will surely be safe with you - til we meet again in whatever world comes after.

All my love,
XXXX

TAXIDERMY POST-BREAKUP

seems you are always trying to make immortal
the death of the transient
butterfly pinned, bones spread wide
marriage rings untarnished by the rot.

will you shun the lover if she doesn't live forever?
do you refuse the wind for moving still?
some things are not eternal & that too is as it should be

how we laughed with feeling
every night with meaning
now time and I pass you by

sometimes things go wrong
darling just hold on
maybe we won't live but life
goes on; and on; and on;

and on:

hold your final breath close
now hold the door of death closed / find me
before I find your last ghost
so the years and tears and years can one day pass me by

TRUST TRADING

I have not enough words for love
and not enough mouth to buy them with.
and are my lips the coin by which to discover?
how am I to travel- to taste these far and distant hearts-
how am I to know what it means to love?

the day will come when what was sold will be given freely again.

but love is love and flesh is flesh
neither same nor shame nor separate
so what are we but something beautiful and undiscovered
my love i am telling you this
& i cannot separate us from what we are
& maybe i don't need to & maybe this will help
come to peace with what has already been decided

our love is a flock of birds moving.

your heartbeat in my hand. your breath and mine
intermingled, weaving:
this is the truth I would like to leave with.
this is the knowledge I would like to leave you with.

here is what no words can say:
our love is a spring river flowing.
our love is autumn sunlight leaving.

may these words be like amber and immortalize the transient.

the beautiful sorrow gentle ache
beloved ocean gap aching chest heartbeat
oh beloved beloved I am empty
my chest is waves water
                              moving
and what of all could be any better than this?
oh the part of me I left with you is calling
like my lips on the shell of your ear and
the siren sea-wind whisper
                              (don't give it back)
beloved, my heart with you
                        don't give it back.

COLD DRY WHITE

my love, where have you gone?
I have lost you in the body next to me.

my lips
on your skin
go unheard

I would that you wake with a kiss, dear one
but we are no longer the princets from the old tales-

I know we are not forever, beloved
but please be brave.
live just a little longer than this.

My beautiful ghost,
you are a dried flower blooming.
you are winter sunlight; here and gone,
cold and longed-for loveliness.

I do not wish for you to return to me, and
one day I will go to where you are.

-from then on you have always been sleeping.
Shall I call your name?
You would not know me now, but here I am.

you are a soft hymn in my heart /
you are a thousand gentle singing
some loss of emotion here in words I am trying
to convey your loveliness

but now you are none of these things.
untouchable cold unspeaking center of loss
/ small false smile dressed up still
buried in my memory and / in memory you will go

oh but here is the beauty that cannot be torn apart
you live in my heart / you will always live in my heart.